My Whole Heart

Written by
Chiandria Beauford

Illustrated by
Tharushi Nanayakkara

Big Thank Yous to some Big-hearted people:

Thank you to the phenomenal team at Sibley Heart Center Cardiology in Marietta, GA, and Dr. Watson for keeping our family well versed in Caleigh's condition and constant care.

Thank you, Children's Healthcare of Atlanta Egleston and Dr. Kanter for a smooth surgery and such thoughtful aftercare.

Thank you, Kids at Heart, for thinking of all the "little extras" for us while admitted to CHOA when we couldn't. Your support and thoughtfulness towards Heart Families while in and out of the hospital does not go unappreciated.

Last but not least, THANK YOU to Caleigh's family, Nana, Pawpaw, Aunts, Uncles, Cousins, and friends for continuously pushing Caleigh and loving her through and through for the special little girl that she is.

References:

1.   Mai CT, Isenburg JL, Canfield MA, et al. for the National Birth Defects Prevention Network. National population-based estimates for major birth defects, 2010-2014. Birth Defects Res 2019; 1– 16. https://doi.org/10.1002/bdr2.1589.

2.   Center for Disease Control

*This book is dedicated to my daughter, Caleigh,
the strongest Heart Warrior I know. Her resilience
and strength were the inspiration for this book. Her story
must be told. May it inspire all the other Heart Warriors out
there to know they are strong, exceptional,
and capable of ALL things.*

My name is Caleigh. When I was just a baby, my parents were told by my doctor that I had a Congenital Heart Defect, known as ASD.

A Congenital Heart Defect, or CHD,
means there is a problem with the way that
my heart was built when I was born.
The specific defect I have is called Atrial
Septal Defect, a hole in the wall of my heart
between the left and right chambers.

But that doesn't slow me down.
I love going to the park,
  playing outdoors,
swimming, playing with my friends,
and learning about everything
at school!

Some days, I have to go to a special doctor called a Cardiologist, his name is Dr. Watson. The cardiologists' job is to know everything about hearts and making sure they're okay! They give me heavy blankets to drape across my body during x-rays.

Then they put this funny feeling gel on my tummy during my echocardiograms.

Sometimes, they even let me listen to my heart with a stethoscope. It can be scary, but Mommy says I'm a tough girl, and she's right.

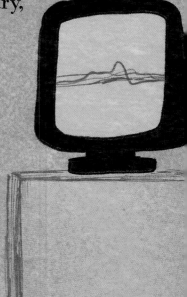

This afternoon, Mommy and Daddy
sat me down to talk about something
called surgery. Daddy says
that means the doctors are going to
go inside my body to fix
my heart and make it like NEW!

Today is my pre-operation day, Mommy says
it will be a long day, but I've got
plenty of paper and markers!
Lots of doctors
come in to talk to Mommy.
They speak for a long while,
but I am ready with my notes.

Here we are! On the day of my surgery, I got this pretty nightgown with all sorts of colorful bears and Mommy and Daddy holding me, giving me lots of kisses. I love that! Here come the nurses! Mommy and Daddy kiss me, "see ya later, Alligator," they say. "Bye-bye, Butterfly," I respond, but I'm pretty sleepy, so I don't think they heard me.

Waking up in a new place can feel a little scary. Seeing Mommy and Daddy right as I opened my eyes made it a lot better. They keep telling me how strong and tough I am! I believe them. But what is this big band-aid here for??

Today I got my room. So many people came by to check on me,
my doctors, nurses, and a big friendly dog!
His name is Uno. We did arts & crafts in the bed,
even went on a scavenger hunt
around the hospital together.

Today is my first full day after surgery. The doctor told Mommy and Daddy, its ok if I want to rest. But NOPE, not me! I want to take a walk around and see my new unit. All the nurses stood down the hallway and cheered me on.
"WOW! She's so strong," one nurse said with a big smile.
"Great Job, Caleigh," said another as she gave me a thumbs up. I feel like a real champion. I know that I am one.

Finally, it's time for me to go home! I can't wait!!
I got balloons, stickers and all kinds of gifts!
But I noticed my band-aid is now gone, and
now there are these
white stickers on my chest.
I'm not sure what they are there for.

Even though my heart is fixed, I still need to go see my doctor to make sure everything is ok. Mommy says something SPECIAL is happening today. I can't wait to see what it is.

DOCTOR

My doctor says he's going to remove my stickers today.
In fact, he says they're not stickers at all.
 They are called steri-strips, and they help
keep my incision closed. He says, not to be worried,
 but there is something very unique
underneath. He takes them off
 one by one. It doesn't hurt at all!

DOCTOR

He finally gets
to the last one.
Mommy yells out,
"A ZIPPER!"
My doctor says a
zipper is a scar left
from heart surgery.
It is only given to
exceptional children
known as
HEART WARRIORS.

WOW!! I'm a real Warrior!
A Heart Warrior! Mommy
and Daddy say I'm basically
a Superhero. I agree!

I hug mommy and daddy because I know
    I am unique, tough, and strong. Just like
they told me I was. As they squeeze me tight,
    I whisper in their ears, "I love you
with my new WHOLE HEART."
        They believe me.

Let's take a look at the heart and what it does!

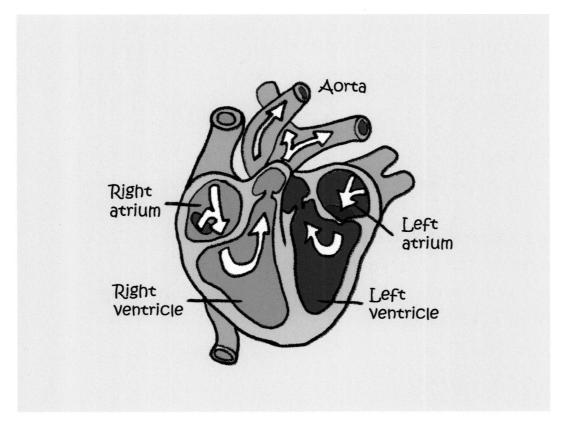

The walls of the heart are made of really strong muscles
that squeeze and relax to pump blood around the body.
This happens about 90 times a minute if you're a child and 70 times
a minute if you are an adult.
Blood is pushed from the atriums into the ventricles
on each side of the heart.

Between them are small valves that open and shut with
each heartbeat so the blood can only flow in one direction.
The main job of the heart is to pump blood to every part of the body.
The blood carries oxygen and all the food, vitamins,
and minerals that your body needs to move, think,
grow and repair itself.

KEY WORDS

- Atrial Septal Defect: An atrial septal defect is a birth defect of the heart in which there is a hole in the wall (septum) that divides the upper chambers (atria) of the heart.

- Cardiologist: a doctor who specializes in the study or treatment of heart diseases and heart abnormalities.

- Congenital Heart Defect: CHDs are present at birth and can affect the structure of a baby's heart and the way it works. These can affect how blood flows through the heart and out to the rest of the body.

KEY WORDS

- Echocardiogram : (echo) is a graphic outline of the heart's movement. During an echo test, ultrasound (high-frequency sound waves) from a hand-held wand placed on your chest provides pictures of the heart's valves and chambers and helps the sonographer evaluate the heart's pumping action.

- Stethoscope: a medical instrument for listening to the action of someone's heart or breathing, typically having a small disk-shaped resonator that is placed against the chest and two tubes connected to earpieces.

- Steri-Strips: surgical tape strips which can be used to close small wounds.

- X-Ray: a photographic or digital image of the internal composition of something, especially a part of the body, produced by X-rays being passed through it and being absorbed to different degrees by different materials.